ALL THE BEST THINGS SHE SAID

Maiche Lev

ALL THE BEST THINGS SHE SAID

by Maiche Lev
All Rights Reserved
Copyright © 2021 HDW Publications

This book may not be reproduced, transmitted, or stored in whole or in part by any means, including graphic, electronic, or mechanical without the express written consent of the publisher except in the case of brief quotations embodied in critical articles and reviews.

Cover and book design by David Bricker
Cover art: "Lady of the Harem" by Edouard Louis Dubufe, c. 1850

ISBN: 978-0-9975757-9-8

Contents

The Cohen Girls 1
He Would Never 3
This is England 5
Love Henry (traditional) 7
Diaphanous 9
And… 11
Rhenfield's Troubled Way 13
I Must Remember 17
Songs are for Singing 19
Visionary 21
A Song for Aviguille 25
"Mean" 29
Betach, Look! 31
Weeping Angel (Shadow on Shadow) 33
Elba South 35
Well-Read, Well-Known 37
Patrice and Ana 39
After All This Time 41
Sure Thing 43
Oh, Michael 45
Saint David's Field 1863 47
Rewards: Another's Ransom 49
Jensen Blue 51
Word 53
Idiot Wind 55

Pleas	57
I Pity You	59
Forever Twenty-One	61
Mississippi Tears	63
Lady	65
And if…	69
In the Next Room	71
Jezebel	77
Write Dreams Down (Closer to the Heart)	81
Where the Honey Come From (Song for Ashley to Sing)	83
How Old Am I?	87
After All That	91
Somewhere	95
Song for Joanne Halayla	97
He's Gonna Win	99
This Maiche, He Uses	101
Envy's Smoked Singe	105
Turnstiles	107
"I'm About Combinations," Said She	109
At Least	111
Rhenfield's Troubled Way (continued)	115
Something Bad	119
Merav	121
I've Known	123
I Am a Rock	125
Afarsimmonim (Persimmons)	127

**ALL THE BEST
THINGS SHE SAID**

The Cohen Girls

I'm not sure…
But I think her first name was Ilana
I saw her here and there on the kibbutz
To see that one smile…
You knew…
Her face had taken centuries to form
She would laugh with her friends
In those green, sandy settings
Her boyfriend was just going to the army
In the months I was there
We never spoke

But unbelievably…
Four years later…
I met a cousin of hers named Merav in New Orleans…
And we laughed at finding that her cousin Ilana
Was known to me
Her beloved relation
And remembering…
I brought up that her cousin had this *smile*
Merav's sweetness could outshine the sun in the sky
But prickly be the Sabra

The Cohen girls
Their voices

Their laughter
Their song
Their freckles from the sun
Hair thick and brown
Their steps
This heritage...

An instinct to protect
The remnants of a people
Prayers eternal

HE WOULD NEVER

It's not what I'd never do, love
It's what I'm not in agreement with
Though tempted I am
The French gal
She's in paradise
The drunken man is at the wheel…[1]
It's not just the tussling of your heart
Deep down it's the tail of something else

"Baby, you know what to do and when…"

---

[1] Bob Dylan, "Dark Eyes" *Empire Burlesque,* Columbia Records, 1985

This is England

In a catwalk jungle
Somebody grabbed my arm
A voice spoke so cold
It matched the weapon in her palm

—Joe Strummer

LOVE HENRY
(TRADITIONAL)

"Hush up, hush up, my pretty parrot," she cried
"And light on my right knee
The doors to your cage shall be decked with gold
And hung on a willow tree"

"I won't fly down
I can't fly down
And light on your right knee
A girl who would murder her own true love
Would kill a little bird like me"

Diaphanous

di·aph·a·nous
dīˈafənəs/
adjective
adjective: DIAPHANOUS
(especially of fabric) light, delicate, and translucent

She wore aquamarine
Open to the hip
Clasped-at-the-ankle
Pants
Diaphanous
Barefoot
In flaming, nighttime, shadowed desert dance
A caravan
A harem's tents
She stood storied above me
Tall enough to squash me like a bug

"Yes, great Sultan…
He's been bothering me for years…"

Under growing shadow…
I woke up

And…

You can believe enough seed spread
Timber choking the soil
Root braiding the ground
Deep shade till dusk…
And dusk dark till dawn

RHENFIELD'S TROUBLED WAY

"I'd give him an Indian"
"What room do you want?"
"Make the mistake"
"Please don't… (burn this house down)"
 Clutching her thigh wrapped in white denim
"Do something!" she bade
"Salt!"
"You'd like to have called"
"Yeah … and I'd like to have lived"
"Who would you rather wake up with?"
 And Gramps said, "I know…"
"I know you love me, David" (a fast swipe in boarding house
   on Carondolet)
"Give me something!"
"I pity you"
"I pity you for your weakness"
 From the parlor in tears
"No … don't wait for me"
"There's your dirtbag…!"
 He heard voices everywhere
"One day she just up and died"
"I'm waiting for you; it's been a month"
 The orchestra
"He's gonna burn everything"
"I've been fisting this woman for 25 years," said he
 Lesser men have committed worse over less

"Don't ever try to change me"
"I've been in this thing too long"
"You'll have to pass through the rings of life," said she
All ten of them?
"Drunk"
"Cute"
"Say hello to all those people in … Ceasarea?
She spoke on 44th street
Heading north on Meridian
Laughing
Wearing rectangular, raspberry glasses
And the twang in Central Park wasn't imaginary
Passing by silver bench
Early November sunshine
Who are you to travel?
He's on some other shore
The sackcloth trundle tumbling downward shifting in space
After hamster marathon #17
Who's counting?

In Denmark
Where I was once a king with three daughters
Kissing is considered infantile
Maybe he's one of those 7–11 people
Wake up, David Weinstein
I'll go easy on ya
You know who you are better now, Merav

It works

(It doesn't work)

Guatemalan blanket

A green one in the lobby laid out in a glass lodge somewhere

I felt like you were way older than me

That's a lot of money

You can afford it

A few more of those…

What was the song Rose sang to the stars while lying
   on the headboard in the frigid North Atlantic?

"Smoke Gets in Your Eyes"

No; it's not that one…

You draw a smile

Jamerson crawling

I Must Remember

I must remember
That every man you've ever been with
Isn't a tyrant or a villain or an enemy
Every position you've found yourself in
Isn't a crime unto creation and all humanity
Your voice and its nudity, m' lady

Pleasure discovered
Vast and varied
Full-on intensity
I, too, maintained realms of pleasure
That came as a relief

There was a time I camped out in your backyard
Set out to blow your mind
The idea that I could make a wave
A salvation of some kind

I've got to stick my head in the sand
Without sticking my head in the sand
Got to overcome these feelings
Felt by every man

I've got to accept that you're gone
To be with another lover

If I read a thousand books...
Y' never really get the feeling
Between a thousand covers

Songs are for Singing

Her flesh is light
White
Orange
Gold
Quietly burning
Eyes set
Fast and slashing
Deep in the night's darkness
Onyx…
Shira

Morocco's Jewess
Absolute riches
Men fear losing her
This'll never come again…

Only a poet knows where he lay
Tears run down temples
Not a word spoken
One candle lit

She keeps you
Songs are for singing
I know one…
But not all that well
Shira

VISIONARY

I've seen a spider in a steel web
I'm not sure…
It may or may not have had a raspberry cap on its head
I've seen a woman made of cream
Climb up a shapeless cast
There were little pin-spots of light
We were in a dark room
She wore a nightgown
And looked into a blowhole at the top
The nightgown wasn't sexy
I think it was off-yellow-white

I saw an old friend's father
Laid back in the clouds
His nose was like a stork's
He seemed to be observing something speculatively…
Confidently
His head was cocked sort of proud
A woman by a mirror said, "We killed him, didn't we?"
Then a man said, "He did something stupid"
In the same space
Months on
The same woman lowered herself to engage herself sexually
    with two men I know
In the corner there by the front window

I can't go on looking in the same cracked mirror shattered
With a board stuck through the bottom rungs
Makes a pretty good bed 'neath this open ladder

What was apparently enough for me…?
What was enough for you?
Well, you've done it all
And there's no more anyone can pretend to do
You played it like you saw it
Again and again
I woke up every morning of my life
Knowing your name
Even if I could seize it all
It seems like an evil deed
I keep finding the word "catastrophe"
Do we need to meet again in this life?
For the love of a house full of children
I don't need to get used to having lost any more
I don't need to spend any more time alone
I do not savor the idea of being a washed-up,
   never-was musician
There is no moment big enough to contain these thoughts
I didn't let the world go by to meet up with this
Didn't cross a desert
Didn't suffer young guns
The most unoriginal sin
Didn't think the deed would press

The Earth is rich and pure in soil dark

Waters fresh

Melting snow

But its poisons are wicked deadly, aren't they…?

She quakes

She rumbles

Her winds they blow

And her winds…

They blow

A Song for Aviguille

She was for me a savior
That's the way it was, yes
Effortless, her way
Collecting and mailing in the same breath

Sort of like a Shelly Duval
Only all would agree
Shelly Duval would've sat in awe
In the back seat

Eyes big and blue
Strawberry blonde
Bow-jawed
Handsome

But a savior…?

Find a companion…
A lover
Passionate about the same music
That rings
Someone who's serious but still fools
Someone who laughs at the same things

Someone who looks into you
And finds the angles she loves

A time we had
A time it was

And you feel it…
Acceptance
Attraction
Vibrance
You're too young and dumb to know you're blessed

You're too young and dumb to know that you're blessed

This backward world
This poisoned place
Tonight someone else looks into her face

The fool you were to have so not recognized
She wore dark blue slacks when the divorced was finalized
Her tone of voice
Now, her tears
You're so full of yourself
And you have been for years

She couldn't have given more
A savior…
A son
And you
The walking wounded
Forever haunted by some former lover

You had a completeness
That would still stand today
To have lived your life with her...
A saving grace
A savior
It was...
"Dry your eyes, my little friend
Let me take you by the hand"[2]

A song for Aviguille

---

2 Zevon, Warren, "When Johnny Strikes Up the Band. "Warren Zevon," Asylum Records, 1975

"Mean"

Mean happens
Mean spreads
Mean
Not to the morgue; just a hospital bed
Mean is a rope
Something wound by many threads
Mean
Irritated
An angry outburst where harm resulted
Mean
A frenzy of ill intention
Mean
Okay children, that's our lesson on meanness
Time for rest period
Mean
Y' gotta keep 'em separated…

Mean as Robert Plant, Axel Rose, and Bon Scott without
 their Dilaudid
Mean as four hurricanes on the ground
Grinding to and through your hometown
Where the barometer plummeted
Raw buffalo heart is probably culinarily "mean"
Serve with coleslaw
Not the sweet, the shredded

What do folks think of when they think of "mean?"
They think of Jaws
Haven't been back in the water since...
Since Martha's Vineyard's Independence Day
 celebration ended
Mean
This or that pornographic scene
Mean
A nice chianti with fava beans

What makes you feel mean?
Behind that curtain is a man controlling a screen
You're doin' it so mean

Betach, Look!

Ezekiel 19:2   What a lioness was your mother
 among the lions!
 Crouching among the great beasts
 She reared her cubs

WEEPING ANGEL
(SHADOW ON SHADOW)

A woman at a desk

Overcome with emotion

Giving into it

Falling on her elbows

Head in her palms

She gave way

She cried

A woman at her desk

A dark shadow dream

I and I

Elba South

On the bus
A student with a transparent knapsack
Blocking your space
Practically in your lap
The L going south
You push him just enough
To let him know you're there
"Excuse me…"
You have shorts on
And diamond studs
I ask you your name…
You don't answer
A less impersonal inquiry there is not
You're scrolling your screen
I should have stolen your phone
And ran out the back door at the next stop
You'd have given chase
And we'd have laughed

Well-Read, Well-Known

The other side of a glorious page
Is there not some dismal dearth…?
Just as sharp as the point of its script
Is a darkness blacker than ink

A page as long and square as it is paper-thin
The title smudged as its lines run clear
Its signature scrawled
Its spine in shreds

You've given your youth
And your health
And your sanity…

"Bookmaker … Nobody reads!"

Patrice and Ana

How do you accept an open marriage, Patrice?
Well, Ana…
He'd do it twice to me if he didn't do it once to you…

After All This Time

After all this time
These distances…
I've never really asked myself how it's been with you

Maiche…
Your voice is as if my own

Sure Thing

Live Aid is a sure thing
Legs all the way down to the ground
Knocked out loaded
I smell Porsche
Citróen
Maserati
Or maybe a cream-colored vintage Vette
A black Ferrari

Let's tail him
And see what kind of trouble we might cause down the line
These things take time
Mmm
The sweet smell of extortion
Dirt! Bring me some dirt!
There's money to be made
And we're gonna make some off this self-righteous fool!

Gilligan strikes again
He's only a man
A chimp in an engineer's cap some say
Something hypocritical
Yes!
Some sin of his holiness
Some mark on his halo

I bet he's a porn freak
Tap his fucking phone already!

I hear there's photographs
Of some real demeaning shit
From what is said to be
Some experimental, ultra-depressed phase
In Tel Aviv from *years* back
Damn! Even the Jews eat their own

Where does he go when he steps from the dais?
Leave the cameras
He'll be back
All men are dirtbags

Yes, call the missus…

OH, MICHAEL

At this moment I feel no love for you at all
I never thought it could happen
But it has
Oh, Michael…

Saint David's Field 1863

Called a thief…
Who left whom to die in there…?
Called a liar…
By one who couldn't go any deeper
With souls who couldn't get any higher

I don't know what you say I never felt…
I lived this … feeling
What was the cocaine for?
The twelve-by-seven-foot cell
Was twelve-by-seven feet tight
It's said that when you reach enlightenment
You bow at the feet of your enemy
I'm not completely wrong
And you're not completely right

And I don't know what you meant when you said, "It isn't fair"
Must be something I don't know
Something I don't understand…
Again…
Who left whom to die in there?

Tumbleweed snowballin'
A bundle tumblin' down a chute
Lieutenant Dunbar missed his cue

Forgot to grab the iodine
And pour it down into his boot

Rewards: Another's Ransom

Would I harm the fruit of your womb?

Not knowingly…
Never
But oh, queen, reining queen
If it is that you have demolished all here standing…
Where might it fall?

Jensen Blue

There was a nun
Who gave birth to ten children…
Soon to be eleven
She'd been tempted
She … herself

There was a cardinal
Who every so often dreamt of woman's form
He prayed to be rid of his sin
He began to relieve himself
He … himself

She *knew* sin from sin
She brought to herself
What was left in his bin
She kept her swell 'neath her habit
No one noticed
She, tall and Slavic
She … herself

The world kept spinning on its axis, it did
The priest kept goin' for fish 'n' chips
And the nun
Like clockwork…
For ten-plus years

She rode his on her hip
She ... herself

Whispered prayers
Through thin lips
Until she was found
And she confessed
And confessed
Asked why she did this
"Because I could, I guess…"

For all his service
He was *excommunicatus*
He always loved the Volkswagen hippie bus
No one knew he could play chromatic harmonicas
He ... himself

The nun…
Her flock was corralled
And once a year there was a jubilee
Can't keep the press away
People write books about her still
She ... herself

WORD

How little we talk
How *much* you know…

Idiot Wind

You'll never know the hurt I suffered
Nor the pain I rise above
And I'll never know the same about you
Your holiness or your kind of love
And it makes me feel so sorry[3]

---

3. Bob Dylan, "Idiot Wind," *Blood on the Tracks,* Columbia Records, 1975

Pleas

Pleas upon pleas
I never feel right before or after
Like news correspondents speaking in the
    first-person omniscient
"I think…"
Dudes with motorcycles run off with the girl
You find you want to fly
But all about you
Whining despots are somehow still learning to crawl
The photos are real…
I was being followed by a girl's spirit
Ever bluffing
Quietly incredulous to herself
(Of course)
I guess my last dream was there
In a distant Louisiana farmhouse
Its front door a high mantle
The sky a perfect pancake of dirty cloud
The words, "You're not a journalist" hung somewhere
    between rooms
This she-pirate
Had she left me slain?
Her blade 'tween her teeth as she swung across?
The sun rose and fell
Then and there

I wore khakis and a professor's shoes

I woke…

Oddly content

Unbothered

And with no lingering fears

I Pity You

It's not embarrassment I feel…

It's loss…

Mine

FOREVER TWENTY-ONE

It's probably for the best
That we remain this way
Practically mythical to one another
Hard lessons too heavy to learn

And not a single intimate conversation all year
Forever twenty-one

Mississippi Tears

God would never be so cruel to make me live
without your face

—Joan Osbourne

LADY

Lady
What is there about me that you'd have to hold?
Tell me, lady
Tell me…
Tell me what you think of when you think of me…
When you think of me to have and to hold

Lady
Haven't we both been cruel?
Haven't we both been sorry?
An ocean of time in between
It's been rough
Topsy-turvy
Busses and trains and elevators
Lifts and sidewalks
Streetcars and trolleys

Lady
What did we really know of each other?
Who can attest to living in the same old dream?
What might I have to give that would work for ya…?
What might that be?
Lady, what might that be?

Bouncin' off of something so special
You'd think a man would remake his world

We'd never get out of bed if we could see the future
Are we at the end of the road?
Out to pasture?
I'm not sayin' I can't forget
I've just never ceased to remember

Lady
I know you'd agree
That no one really learns to be alone
To talk about drained cups and torn clothes
The seal read, "Something shrewd nets many believing"
Who could no longer spin in a mobile of grieving?

Lady
Ladyfinger
Lady Luck
Lady longing
Lady looking
Lady love
Something tells me I'm in the kind of trouble
There's no getting out of

Lady
I'm in another town
One where you are not
Is there a man alive who's put himself through this much?
A hollow tree's rot

A soldier's tourniquet
You may have heard different
But I don't get out much
That's the understatement of the year
Lady, ask God
He might send you here ...

I've got to move 'cause I can't stand still
The first time ever I saw a hummingbird
It was through the screen
In an infirmary's window sill
Little boy...
You just like being picked up by a pretty nurse
Back to the cabin, little man

Lady
One plus one is almost two
What of yours have I never belonged to?
Lady of the forest
Lady of the river
Lady of the sky
The moon
Stranger
Let's just go get a room

Chelsea
Picture an island in a stream

Are you a partner of mine
Or are we just keeping company?

What of me would you have to hold?
Tell me…
This song is what I think of when I think of you, lady
What do you think of when you think of me?
Warm?
Cold?
Calm?
Crazy?
Lazy?
Pretty boy, Brad Paisley?
You love me
You play me
You kill me
You slay me

Lady…

AND IF...

And if he's winning
You must…
And if he's smart
You will…
And in the blandest voice
"Hit him"

IN THE NEXT ROOM

She said, "At last, a human…
And such a cute one"
Gets the job done
A lot of fun
Lots of friends…
Musicians
He's a playboy … and where have *I* been?
I like his father
His spirited daughter
His beauteous son
They listen
With an air of respect and discipline
Their heritage…
Like mine…
Judaism
They point out to one another things they need to "work on"
He's surprisingly sweet without misplaced affection
So much that's accessible under his roof…
I think I'll marry him

There was something about you, Ravi, that I loved
Just like you said the same of me
For one brief day I was the man for you
All those years ago in that Louisiana sun
My job seems to be living this failure

They can talk about me plenty when I'm gone
It all seems like a long time ago
It has been
I have not served myself well
I'm guilty of hesitation

I've lived a life of hesitation
We're all ruled by the powers we've clung to…
What is it about that Mississippi River?
That Louisiana jurisdiction?
I missed the mark
Overstepped the line
My strung-out way of thinking
And how I've lost you this way
My heart's only prayer
My pen
My song
The pulse of its vacillation
Your love
Something never my own
Yes…
Yes, a profound deprivation

Am I sorry I ever met you?
I'm not capable of the declaration
Do I hate you?
Should I?

The issue of transcendent annihilation
I've hidden myself away
To find someone
I've worn you as my own skin
Duck-duck-goose in heaven

Sounds funny but it isn't
It's a terrifying notion
What I'm saying is…
I've woken up with you
And worshipped the thought of you far, far too long
Inescapably an outrageous misfortune
And I let this continue
And all this useless pain was reduced to a radio show
  about men
Obsessed men as something pathetic and merely bothersome
Heard it in Pensacola in my kitchen
How some boyfriends like this feel owed a love for their
  undying devotion
For their art
Their emotion
Their bitchin'

Really…
I've got a feeling now that a lot of women out there
Are the *right* women
It's just taken me thirty years to come out the other end

Yeah, the right woman…
She's gonna light up New York after a blackout
Like a southern town a week after a hurricane
Like … a weight that's been lifted
Like something
Like someone human

We were put together but it was not to be
I've got to land and walk and find my way without
    thought of failure
And so I can
And so I will
Deep breath
I'm bound away
And you have lived a life more full than any
I can't resent a thing
I'd only be further ripping myself off
In the last few days I've thought of your voice in that bathtub
That clawfoot old fashioned bathtub
Too good to be true
And the rest pretty much a pity

Pretty much a pity….
And it became pretty much a joke
Me in the next room
Paper and pen
Raising my hand
Declaring "Alas!"

And you in the next room
Falling on your face
With the lucky and famous
Listenin' to the mother of God sell her ass
Ancient justice
The sexes
The sex's politics
I do not expect that in my times of trouble
You'll be there for me
When you know a pang of emptiness
Out in the wilderness…
Beat a path of retreat
Up them spiral staircases
Past the tree of smoke
Past the angel with four faces
Begging God for mercy
And weepin' in unholy places
Angelina…[4]

Mamounia mamounia mamounia
Species
Breeds
Races…

In the next room
The keeper of the keys

4 Bob Dylan, "Angelina" Studio Outtake. *The Bootleg Series Volumes 1-3 (Rare & Unreleased) 1961-1991.* Columbia Records, 1991.

In the next room…

Me

On the road to Beit Shemesh

Twisted from Ein Kharem past the small rock quarry
   by the Canadian forest

The fork toward Jenin

And Nazareth led to that 45-degree drop

The asphalt lay as though drip-dried

A road sign for Bethlehem somewhere in there

I fell so far I didn't think I'd make it back[5]

And your cousin's smile on Tzora was something to live for

In the next room at Achziv

The classy couple left something behind…

Eli didn't ask me to clean it up

I used a rag

Like it was the most natural thing in the world

Waved up at the F-22 jet fighter

Moving slowly

900 feet overhead

---

5 Matthew Sweet. "Smog Moon," *100% Fun.* Zoo Entertainment, 1995

JEZEBEL

It's like maybe there are three of you
Maybe four
No … not any less but maybe more
I'm not entirely sure

One is an understanding being
With wisdom beyond her years
That I ever knew her at all…
Gets me right here…

One is someone else
Weighing purpose
Once astonished
Once fraught

You're a bowl of milk
You're a barrel of monkeys
You're a band of thieves
You're a wide glass of pink Chablis

One is incensed
Angry
Severe
Saying little
Intimidating
Is Jezebel someone to fear?

One is conniving
At what is she driving?
That devil
Snickering
Bickering
Cold
Calculating
Anything but on the level

In one…
You're the face of a playing card
The queen is garbed
Staring deadpan
Almost holy
Is anyone home?
She's no one's one and only
Jezebel

In another you're perfect as a mango
I actually thought of that not long ago
A ripe, juicy mango
With oranges and yellows and reds
I actually thought of that…
Do I really walk around all day
With the image of this woman in my head?

In one…
Well, gee…

Who's this monkey?
T h e   l a s t   c h i m p a n z e e ?
And sittin' right next to me
Scratchin' her belly
You can tell if a chimp's happy or sad
Thoughtful
Angry
Randy
Crazy!
Mad!
Bananas?

Oh, this one is a spirit of the desert
A horse who won't obey her thirst
Hiawatha
Pocahontas
Jasmine
Ariel
Sarah
Sharon
Leah
Rachel
Rebecca

Jezebel!

WRITE DREAMS DOWN
(CLOSER TO THE HEART)

Ravi was there
With her final surgery exposed
In a can
She with her tight hairline
Sat in back of me on a train
The next day
In this dream the walls were blue
Like the Blue Grotto restaurant in New York City
Their specialty
Chicken scaparelli
Amoebic figures
Like bent skateboards on the wall
Colors mixed into them like dark rust
Like dried blood
No windows
Two queen-sized beds
Adjoined
A figure that might have been me
Was like a ghost in hysterics
His face pressed up against the wall
I left and returned
And snuggled up to take her anally as offered
But it all petered out
And I got up and looked around
The feeling of threat prevailed

No one had bathed in quite some time
A younger person came in
And Rene Russo the actress
I penetrated her vaginally
Someone walked by with a black-haired infant
Who had arms like black sticks
A voice said
"He's riding chemotherapy"
A voice said something...
I don't remember...
Bit it felt like the scene knew a defendant
Someone said someone had a bunch of little stories...
The heart of my being was locked into Ravi
But the filth everywhere
Made me cautious and paranoid
And then someone mentioned being stabbed in the heart
A white Mercedes
With a personalized license plate that said
"NO MYSTERY"
And then...
Before the dream ended
I spoke the words
"I'm not your friend today
Nor will I be tomorrow"
And then...
Someone asked "Who fell?"
And another replied, "You've been revealed"

—'21 Delrey Cottage

WHERE THE HONEY COME FROM
(SONG FOR ASHLEY TO SING)

I met this guy
Kinda shy but he could sing
Tuned up my ukulele for me
Replaced a string
I didn't know how sweet a boy could be
We were singing our birthday song
All about where the honey come from

I met this guy
Totally gone
Totally gone in every way
In the fields of the university
So young and handsome
Hiding from the librarian
He didn't need a book or a lesson
He knew where the honey come from

I met this guy
He was older and wise
Treated me like I was the queen of Dubai
When I was bad he spanked my royal bum
He knew where the honey come from

I met this guy with tiger's eyes and tiger's claws
He sniffed me with his nose

He pawed me with his paws
The sound of growling in my ears
Animal magnetism
Sniffing around where the honey come from

I met a guy who was going too slow
Wouldn't let go
Nearly lost my mind
I met a guy who was going too fast
I couldn't get past
Nearly lost my mind
Too fast
Too slow
Wouldn't wish it on anyone
Takes two to tap where the honey come from

I met a guy who had a girl named Penelope
He introduced her to me
Then we were three
They say lust is a sin
Honeycomb
Honey cake
Honey bun
We got so sticky
Couldn't come undone
That's where…
That's where…
That's where the honey come from

I met a guy
A divorcé
And I'll tell you absolutely
He stroked my body
Loved me to tears
He did; did he?
My memory of the event
Shall we say is … foggy
Paid me every attention
Made me keep my glasses on
He knew where the honey come from

I met this guy
Rocket scientist
He *invented* the Rubik's cube
Wore thick black glasses
Pencil neck
Perfect gentleman from day number one…
He knew where the honey come from

How Old Am I?

How old am I?
I'm old enough to strike back
Tear out the floor
Slash your tires for fun
Old enough to burn a house down with you in it
I'm old enough to sleep on nails
Old enough to look right through you
Old enough to lose to win
Old enough to put down a foot of pride
To turn despair on its side
Old enough to know where you've been and what y'
    been doin'

How old am I?
Old enough to wish I'd started a whole lot sooner
Old enough to dust my broom
I'm covered in the dust of rumor

How old am I?
Old enough to dig a well
You will not be seeing me in hell
Old enough to blow up my TV
Smash my radio
An army of one
Are you talkin' to me?

Some love is a drop in the ocean
I don't have two words for *anyone*
Old enough to know all the friends I ever had are gone

How old am I?
It's too late to die young
The good guys didn't win
It was the bad guys who won

Old enough to know
Sometimes someone wakes up in a scream
Old enough to know
What a "snake in the grass" means
Old enough to know
Vengeance is sweet
Old enough to say
"I'm sorry…
But I can't accept your apology"

How old am I?
Old enough to know I've been a fool
Old enough to know I've been taken to school
Old enough to know y' don't know what you've got till
  it's gone
Angel of morning
I'm old enough to face the dawn[6]

---

[6] Dusty Springfield, "Angel of the Morning" *Goin' Back — The Definitive Dusty Springfield.* Lyrics by Chip Taylor. Mercury Records, 2011

Old enough to know that craving leads to tears
Old enough to know you can miss out on something long hoped for
Old enough to know that despair has its own behaviors
When you've got no game
You've got no measure
It's true…
So true
How true?
What's true?

Old enough to know what it feels like to have to let things lie
People will walk all over you
To live and let live
To live and let die

I have only come here seeking knowledge
Y' learn more in a day of kindergarten
Than y' do in four years of college

How old am I?

After All That

After all that
What goes on in the course of a day is still so unreal
After all that
To stay until my rivers run dry
Disraeli Gears
How must *that* feel?

Dirty deals
Broken seals
Have you a gripe of some kind?
The other day I saw some kids
Spray-painting a question mark on a "Dead End" sign

"What am I most sorry for?" she began to ask herself
I'll show him…
He'll feel this for the rest of his life!
No one passes through here unscarred
I'll show him…
He thinks he's Bob Dylan!

All your love…
Cost y' all your love
No ifs, ands, or buts
It *will*…
Not it *might*
Some things *do* cost you *all* your love

A man can only take so many blows
Before he goes down
And down he stays
And they're pretty sure they know why
They're dancin' on his grave…
Pretty sure

This you did, you Godless creature!
This you did and did again
Twice the swamp cried, "Help me!"
Back some time ago…
I don't remember when

And Coco's boy puts his two cents in:
Why are we still even talkin' about him?
You were on your deathbed
And half-drunk, he brought in balloons
I hear he brought a boom-box to a funeral
And broke out some writing at a wake
Don't let him tell you for *one second*
You've done anything inappropriate
Guy's the ultimate fuckin' hypocrite
When I think of 'im I get *sick*

I know her too well
Here…
I've written another song about it

Well…
It was senseless…
Highly insensitive
I'm sorry…
It was downright rude and fuckin' ugly
And just plain tawdry
Deadly
Incorrigible
Without restraint
Out of control
Irreligious
Seditious to the commonwealth
Beyond protocol
Clueless
Spineless
Thoughtless
Surprising…
I can't believe it
It's a crime; he should be shot!
The gall
The pair he's got!

He misses someone he missed…
And he's missed her so long
He's poisoned…
As poisoned as gone

I'll show him…
I'll show him again

Somewhere

You were sitting alone
Peaceably staring off
And he came over and said
"You're talking with him"
And you replied
"I love him"

Song for Joanne Halayla

He would never...
Said Miss Lucy to Mister Jinks
No...
He would never disrespect the living
Nor trespass on the dead
Many tongues only flatter or belittle
But cannot speak

He's Gonna Win

He's gonna win
That makes you the prize
Please show me to the d-d-door
Before I gouge out my eyes

He's gonna win
That makes you the prize
The pain is not acute
It radiates
It's generalized

Your ways have broken many a heart
And mine is surely one
Y' gotta watch what y' say to a woman
And she's gotta watch what she does to a man

He's gonna win
You're the prize
I missed the mark
Overstepped the line
Yes, it hurts to realize
Her ribbons
Her braids
Her accent
A prize

Was that a woman?
Yes, it was
In every way
In every sense of the word
Every inch
Every stitch
Every look
Every curve

He's gonna win
You're the prize
The rest is salt and sand
Angel heart
Angel eyes

My sadness will pass
As my senses will rise
Yes…
My sadness has passed
My senses arise

This Maiche, He Uses

He uses dead butterflies
And red leaves

He uses fabrics he's found
Wrapped around Stevie Nicks posters
Bella Donna

He uses superglue
He glued the keyhole of my husband's motorcycle lock
An Indian
(Not the ignition)

He uses magnets from board games
Stuck to our doorway's metal gate off Decatur
He's yet to throw a rock through the antique glass
I'd kill him!
Dead!

This Maiche…
Glitter
He's a grown man in Hobby Lobby
Or Michael's
That's emasculating!

He tosses half-eaten Granny Smith apples
By the mailbox buzzer box thing

When he's back in town
Green apples
My favorite

This Maiche tapes the key to his room on Carondolet Street
Beneath a scale model of a '67 cream-colored Corvette
Keeper!

He uses Gordon Lightfoot sheet music tied with
   a black ribbon

He uses books with their covers torn off

He left ginger candies
So hot I called him a sick sonofabitch!

He sent me a raggedy, torn-up video cover
Of *Debbie Does Dallas*
I framed it

Once he took everything the color green in his apartment
And jammed it through the wrought-iron bars
Green pens and markers
A green tee-shirt
A green dress shirt
Chopsticks wrappers
Paper clips

An athletic cup!
Green chalk
Green crayon
And then another green apple in February
A miniature Yoda
Mine!
Plastic folders
A scrub-brush
A decaf coffee package
A Phisoderm® bottle

This man brought to New Orleans
Three duffle bags
And a suitcase full of his original writing
One morning we came out
And a thick carpet of his work blanketed the moon

He sent me a poster of vinyasic yoga positions
All the moves revealed by a yoga master named Hanuman
Cover-to-cover
All of it
Well…
Turns out I know Hanuman from the posters
Top five of my wildest lays in this life
You heard me
A mountain goat
Evil!

Maiche uses spray-paint at will
And epoxy
And Maiche…
Don't ya push me baby…

Someone… painted the bottom of his Pumas
And walked up and down this street for five days
Get off my lawn!

He makes ribbons out of paper bags
He makes swans out of paper clips
Nothing says "love" like stalking

I love you, Maiche
Ring the bell
I'm waiting for you, boy…
We could burn the midnight oil

Envy's Smoked Singe

Envy's smoked singe
Jealousy's lash
Irony's scorch
Honesty's blow
Denial's clutch
Vanity's rib
Resentment's fire
Hatred's stake
Innocence lost
Eminence front
Confession's scraps
Imagine rain

Turnstiles

She will haunt you
It was how things dawned on her
That you marvelled at…
Fool

"I'm About Combinations," Said She

"I'm about combinations"
And all those fun little medications
How's it gonna be
When you have to pay
For what's always been free
If I'm not mistaken...
If I haven't been forsaken...
Your namesake is sleeping 'neath the 77th Street
   lifeguard station
I've been double-crossed now for the very last time
And now I'm finally free
I kissed goodbye the howling beast
On the borderline which separated you from me[7]
There are those you can tell will never be judged
Empathy...
Please walk all over me
I've brought you roses
And a box of Riverwalk fudge
Hung out to dry
A raw deal
We're made of dreams till the end
"Au revoir, Cheridon
Au revoir"
I'll go to Crete if Lebanon is closed

---

7. Bob Dylan, "Idiot Wind," *Blood on the Tracks,* Columbia Records, 1975

And here comes that truck with the well-trained dalmatian
Still soapy from his bath
Nowhere to bury his nose

AT LEAST

At least she was alive
Said Ol' Boss Hogg to Brother Love
Stage right
Stage left
You guys…

At least she was alive
Alive
Living
Breathing here
I never got as close as anywhere near

At least she was alive
I woke up empty…
Wiped…
Done…
The night so gay wore on and on
Where men practiced the hoax of free speech
And bathed in cheap perfume

At least she was alive
Someone said
They'd both be better off dead"
Who'd she take her orders from?
Who were the mud-caked creatures
Lyin' in her bed?

At least…
She said the secret was rhythm
Said she wasn't feelin' it
She called for a mini-surrender
What was I doing that you felt so threatened by?
Why do I need a fucking excuse to be literate?
Bad news
Sad news….
Came to me in my sleep…
A crime is committed when something royal is made cheap

I don't know from calling bluffs
I don't know from knowing better
Keep your babble
And your riddles
Mister Jinks and Ms. Lucy
Were not people of letters
No…

At least she was alive
The things you see at parties…
Stuck with her, they did
If there are only twelve types of souls in the world…
How it feels when you find someone's cast your lot
Bid your bid
Congratulations on your New Jersey wedding
It's time for me to slide

Sadly enough
To be rid...

At least she was alive
She could do anything the boys could do...
Even better
She made a monkey out o' me
And don't y' know I let her!

At least she was alive
News come down the line
One day she up and died...
She sure crammed in a lot of livin' in her years
Don't know what role I played...
We never walked hand in hand
We never laid in each other's arms
We never spoke
And one day she up and died...
Like no man knows

At least she was alive

RHENFIELD'S TROUBLED WAY
(CONTINUED)

Someone said, "I hate … hate Paul McCartney"
And something about new dreams
And you're an old man
And I'm obsessed with you?
And that an entire library was full of lies
Girls were "bitches"
You gotta do what y' gotta do
A drunk favorite
"She killed it," so did he speak
CD cover bar counter top
Gimme some of that dust
Moocher…
Blame
He did something stupid
And your reply to this was…?
"What kind of husband…?"
Daddy calls me a sinner
His girl calls me a saint
I'm done
Charity is supposed to cover up a multitude of sins
While we're young…
Genius
Gene-Yus!
Best wife I never had

She's a grifter
Come here…
You can taste her ass, man
We're jus' hangin' out
Never be royals
Masochist
You're a sadist
Well … I guess I'm famous
How old are you?
Whose fall?
A toothbrush drying in the sun
Problems with ants
This must be the kicker
He's a pussy!
You don't really believe in this stuff…?
Electric guitars
What is not for public knowledge
Sand man!
Fools
You just kind of groove with it…
Makes me shiver to think about it…
The electricity in a tab of LSD
Moody dude high school
He's lost
Automatic Venus sex freak
He's an assassin
The cat's name is, "Tuesday"

Free radical

I don't do that

(Decals on resin pillars)

Must 've not had enough to do

Where's the remote?

A little bad press…

Turn him loose

Let him go

Let 'im say he outdrew me fair and square

I want him to know what it's like…

Something Bad

"Oh, he must have done something *bad*..."
"I know he's a failure"

Woman is essentially a selfish creature, lad
Look ... she's overshot her exit

MERAV

Merav had that smile
That could outshine the sun in the sky
Through her I learned
You can't forever keep your head in the clouds
That is … to be elusive to your own story untold
I loved this Jewish woman
I loved her to death
Which is no way to spend thirty years of your life
There is no doubt a mysterious shadow in my genealogy now
No doubt
Her string of allegiances in that short-order history
Will serve up a tall glass of ice water
Next to your liver and onions
Your steak and eggs
Your corned-beef hash
And more and more green eggs and ham
There's a bottle behind the jukebox
Waitresses with broken noses…
New Year's Day
Whole town's in bed
I still can't remember all the best things she said
So long, Cheridon
Au revoir

I've Known

I've known jealousy
I've known shame
I've had regrets
I've cast blame

And I've known love
I've known lust
I've known only what's above
And at the bottom … gone bust

I've known stillness
I've known dance
I've known silence

I've known joy
I've known tears
There was a girl when I was a boy
I've been minus that sweetness for too many years

I've known the feelings a man can feel
What success and failure both reveal

"You're surprising"
A voice said unto me

And there was more
But it's escaped my memory

What a grand thing is writing poetry…

I Am a Rock

Don't talk of love
I've heard the word before
It's sleeping in my memory
I won't disturb the slumber of feelings that have died
If I never loved I never would have cried

— Simon and Garfunkel

Afarsimmonim (Persimmons)

Lulu…
Child…
Are you done?
Louise!
I went to him on several occasions!
He stood
He froze
He hid
He bolted
I knew anger would be all he had left…

Child
You know too much of my life
He's married to sorrow
He's downcast
Bereft
He can't imagine a life other than the one he's living
Other than the one he creates for himself

I didn't like his cowering, Lulu
I became an abstract…
An ab-strac-tion to him
I am the object of his heart's desire
But he won't make a move
Or speak a word
I was met by silence

And by silence again
What I did to *him*...
My life, too, unfolded without *someone*
In our brief time together
I can't remember two conversations

You know, Lou...
You know I'm not a chaste woman
I don't apologize for my wealth and success
And I don't apologize for my sexuality
America's about breaking the equilibrium...
The status quo
And I shook it up here!
Where I come from
Freedom is not a given
Time's not for wastin'
On either side of Jerusalem

Louisiana m' love...
I took this man's withdrawn state for a weakness
For the weakness that it was
And then I rode away
I once saw him in a reggae band on South Beach
They played the old stuff all night
His voice filled the space
There he was
Stage right

He used hard drugs for years
I've always encountered him by himself
Alone
In dreams
Alone
On the streets
Alone
In Louisiana thirty years ago
He was a boy with an old mandolin
(That's the little one, right?)

Louise
Baby, there's always half a war goin' on
I did some things that weren't me…
And then…
Because I could
I did 'em again
I was…a menace
Reckless
Even ruthless
Naturally
I'm a woman
There was a hand to play
And why not by l'il ol' me?
He was slighted
Personally
Which was how I meant it to be

Louise
Women are trouble
Intrinsically
Yes, I was reckless
We're attracted to trouble…
Laughter
And cruelty

My life…
Other mothers are victorious in mini-vans
Where I landed here in the States
I could never…
In a thousand years
Have foreseen or planned
These men I've known
From around the world
Intensely firm yet gentle
I find men to be playful
Temptable
And powerful
And women…
Beautiful
Sensual

My indulgences have been like little science projects
And me…
I was havin' babies
While this monk washed his own clothes

And stood over a sink full of dishes
Incredible
Unbelievable

Lulu…
I've made some bad moves
And real mistakes that hurt me still
A part of growing up, child
Is knowing that some things always will

In his writing
He got a lot right…
And he got a lot wrong
When I read him
I'm amazed his mind's still there after so long
And I'm put off that he sat on his poetry
Seems all he's ever done is write

I saw him once years later
On a busy sidewalk in New Orleans
He's filled with dread
And it's left him … undone
Your father is a sad man
He's a kid on a bicycle
In cutoffs with drumsticks
And I'm the Chairman of the Board of an international
    trading conglomerate
And mother of a dozen

At a concert last April
I saw him again
Sitting in the street
Eating an eggroll
Alone of course
Around Jazzfest time
I would have said, "Hello"
But it's like my voice would alarm him
Which is kind of …
Perversely…
Tempting, Loulah
Maybe he needs to be bum-rushed

I don't know, Mom

Lulu…
My 'ouisy girl
It's been so long since I talked to anyone about him
How in this world do people live in each other's dreams?
There's a gripping of the hearts when we meet
And he turns away
It's maddening!
He lives in need of me and I don't know why

My 'ouisy girl
Yes…
So long since I talked to anyone about him
How in this world *do* people live in each other's dreams…?

Maybe I took lovers to forget
Soon after we knew each other
He flew to The Land and made his attempt
In more than a handful of dreams we've met
A poet can live for greater disappointment
His head has always been full of the other-worldly
Things Messianic

There's plenty to dwell on here
If you want to dwell on it
Soulmates
Like some migraine headache

Habibi…
Men and women differ in ways primal
Winds within winds
Strong backs and calloused hands
In our most bizarre hidden places
I can't believe I just said that to my daughter!

Neither can I, Ima…

Lulu…
He's your father
Maybe it's like this…
He's become my angel
And me … his
Our ideas of each other are too pure…

And just the opposite — corrupted and broken
It's what time does
Too close was too far
And too far had no echo
We've made war on each other
In dreams a hundred times
Our tears fell on chalk marks
On as many floors
I, the shapely, shorty extrovert
And he…
A statue
A ghost
Always crumbling
We even managed to get a few good kicks in at the end
Tomorrow is another day…
Just another day

You know I'm a big fan of his
Shyster that he is
So…
You have my love, child
And you know that always and forever
What *most* this scoundrel
He and I shared
Was always all about you, dear Louise

Louise, my love
Sometimes the hardest thing to do is the easiest thing of all

Did I ever show you the shoes I got around the time
   I knew Maiche?
Yes, really…
I've hardly worn 'em
They're ancient
I think they're in the attic
Twenty-seven laces
Ankle high
Gray-blue
With an inch-and-a-half heel

Louise…
Come on…
We're gonna make such a mess…

Ha'ina 'ia mai ana ka puana
Ha'ina 'ia mai ana ka puana[8]

---

8 Native Hawaiian: "It has been said; so it is."

www.ingramcontent.com/pod-product-compliance
Lightning Source LLC
Chambersburg PA
CBHW031150160426
43193CB00008B/319